SCHOLASTIC
Learning Express

Alphabet and Handwriting

This book belongs to

Do Not Write In Book

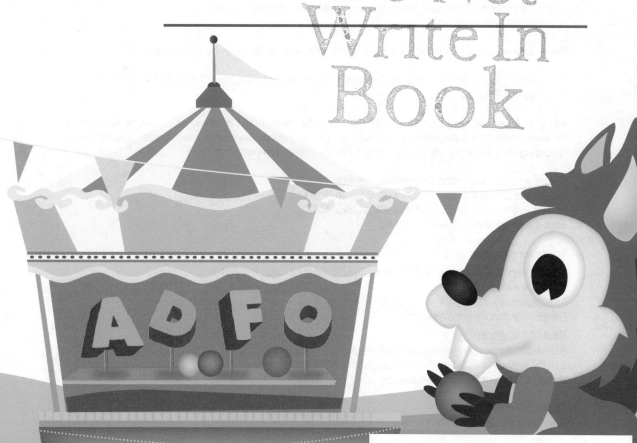

© 2012 Scholastic Education International (Singapore) Private Limited
A division of Scholastic Inc.

Previously published as Reading & Math Jumbo Workbook Grade K by Scholastic Inc.

This edition published by Scholastic Education International (Singapore) Private Limited
A division of Scholastic Inc.

For information regarding permission, write to:
Scholastic Education International (Singapore) Pte Ltd
81 Ubi Avenue 4, #02-28 UB.ONE, Singapore 408830
Email: education@scholastic.com.sg

For sales enquiries write to:
Latin America, Caribbean, Europe (except UK), Middle East and Africa
Scholastic International
557 Broadway, New York, NY 10012, USA
Email: intlschool@scholastic.com

Rest of the World
Scholastic Education International (Singapore) Pte Ltd
81 Ubi Avenue 4 #02-28 UB.ONE Singapore 408830
Email: education@scholastic.com.sg

First edition 2012
Reprinted 2012, 2013, 2014

ISBN 978-981-07-1353-9

Welcome to Learning Express!

Helping your child build essential skills is easy!

These teacher-approved activities have been specially developed to make learning both accessible and enjoyable. On each page, you'll find:

Focus skill
The focus of each activity page is clearly indicated.

Meaningful learning
Each activity has been carefully designed to make your child's learning meaningful and fun.

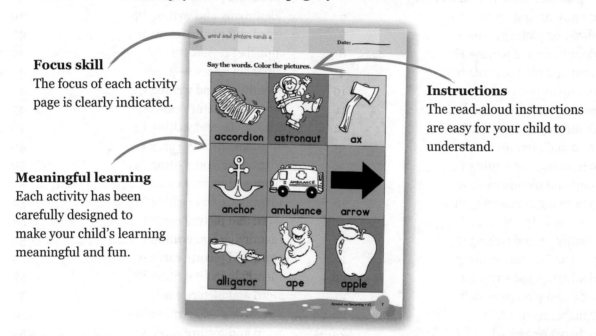

Instructions
The read-aloud instructions are easy for your child to understand.

This book also contains:

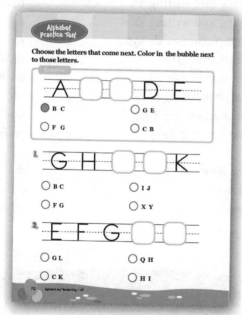

Instant assessment to ensure your child really masters the skills.

Completion certificate to celebrate your child's leap in learning.

Motivational stickers to mark the milestones of your child's learning path.

Contents

Alphabet and Handwriting

"Look, mom, I can write the alphabet!" What a delightful thing to hear your child say. In this book, your child will practice writing upper and lowercase letters of the alphabet.

What to Do
Have your child use a pencil to trace and then write each letter. Next, help your child identify and write words that start with that letter. He or she might choose words from the word and picture cards.

Invite your child to color the pictures. Review the flash cards frequently to help your child develop his or her vocabulary skills during the year.

Keep On Going!
- As you drive or walk with your child, point out signs around the neighborhood. Have your child identify the letters on the signs. Then together, say the words.
- While reading a magazine or the newspaper, encourage your child to look for words on the page that begin with a particular letter, such as B. Then, circle the words.

I am learning about the letter A a.
This is how I write it:

Paste the
Aa sticker
here.

Write two words that start with the letter A a:

_____   _____

-          -

_____   _____

This is my picture of an _____ .

Date: _____

Say the words. Color the pictures.

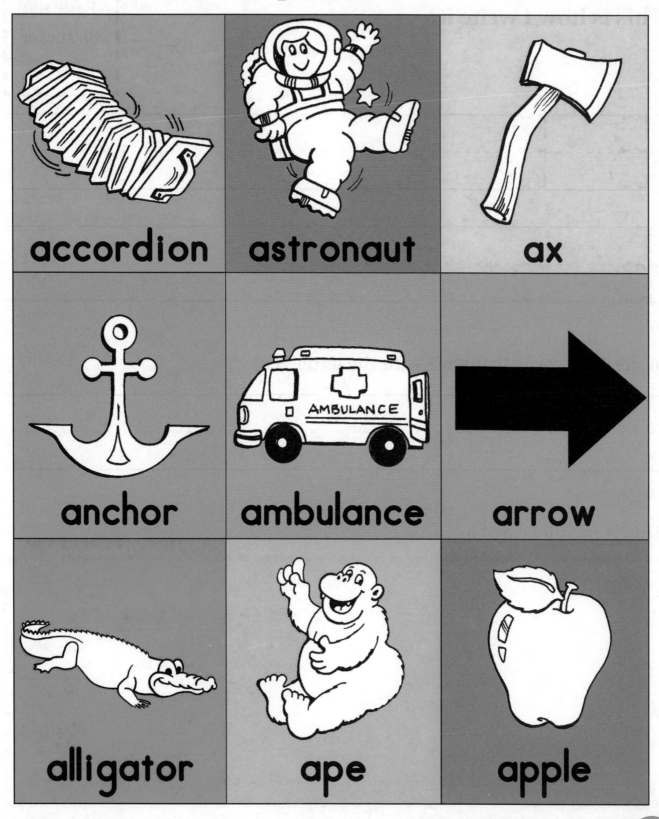

accordion   astronaut   ax

anchor   ambulance   arrow

alligator   ape   apple

Date: _____

I am learning about the letter B b.
This is how I write it:

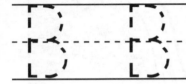

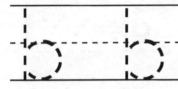

Write two words that start with the letter B b:

_____   _____

- - - - - - - - - - - - - - - - - -   - - - - - - - - - - - - - - - - - -

_____   _____

This is my picture of a _____ .

Say the words. Color the pictures.

balloon	ball	boat
bicycle	bed	book
baby	butterfly	bird

Date: _____

I am learning about the letter C c.
This is how I write it:

Write two words that start with the letter C c:

_____   _____

- - - - - - - - - - - - - - - - - -   - - - - - - - - - - - - - - - - - -

_____   _____

This is my picture of a _____ .

Date: _____

Say the words. Color the pictures.

crab

cactus

cake

calendar

car

caterpillar

cone

cup

corn

Date: _____

I am learning about the letter D d.
This is how I write it:

Paste the
Dd sticker
here.

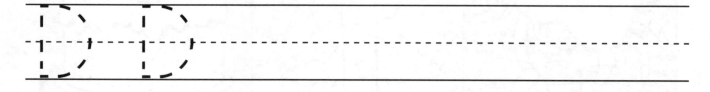

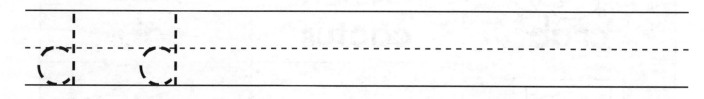

Write two words that start with the letter D d:

_____   _____

-     -

_____   _____

This is my picture of a _____ .

Say the words. Color the pictures.

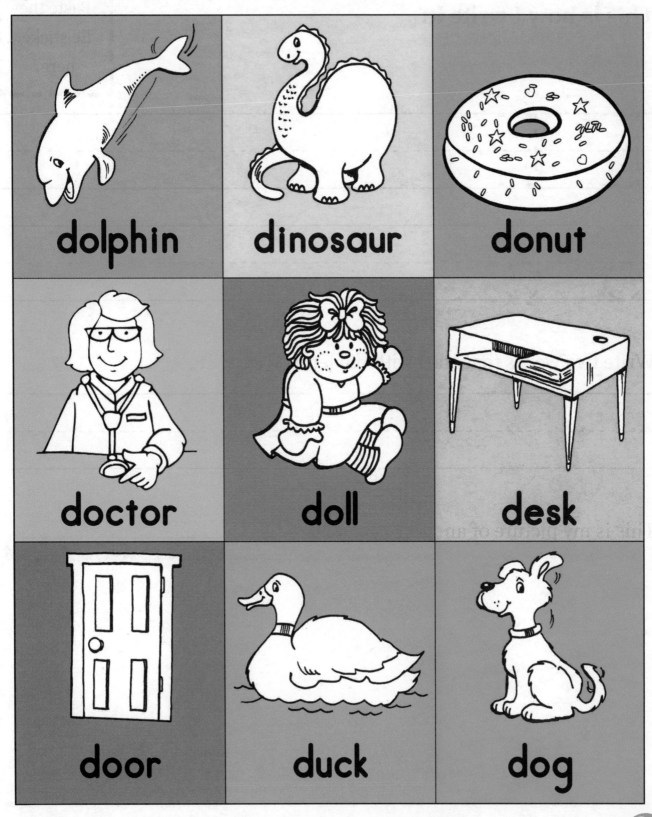

dolphin

dinosaur

donut

doctor

doll

desk

door

duck

dog

Date: _____

I am learning about the letter E e.
This is how I write it:

Paste the
Ee sticker
here.

Write two words that start with the letter E e:

_____   _____

- - - - - - - - - - - - - - -   - - - - - - - - - - - - - - -

_____   _____

This is my picture of an _____ .

Date: _____

Say the words. Color the pictures.

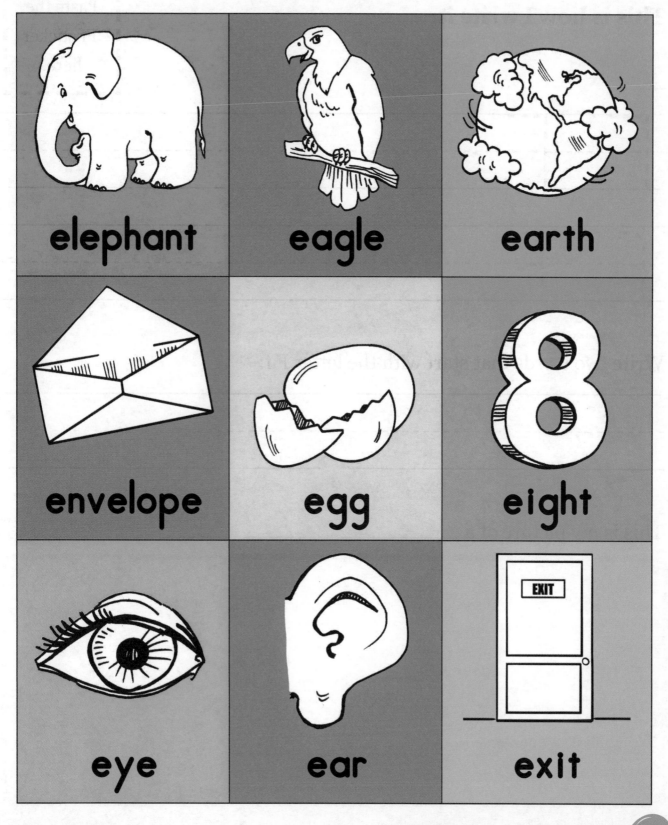

elephant

eagle

earth

envelope

egg

eight

eye

ear

exit

Date: _____

I am learning about the letter F f.
This is how I write it:

Paste the
Ff sticker
here.

Write two words that start with the letter F f:

_____   _____

_____   _____

This is my picture of a _____ .

Say the words. Color the pictures.

fan	feet	fox
finger	five	feather
fish	fire	fork

I am learning about the letter G g.
This is how I write it:

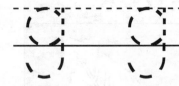

Write two words that start with the letter G g:

_____   _____

- - - - - - - - - - - - - - -   - - - - - - - - - - - - - - -

_____   _____

This is my picture of a _____ .

Date: _____

Say the words. Color the pictures.

game

gate

gift

giraffe

girl

goose

glass

goat

guitar

Date: _____

I am learning about the letter H h.
This is how I write it:

Write two words that start with the letter H h:

_____   _____

- - - - - - - - - - - - - - -   - - - - - - - - - - - - - - -

_____   _____

This is my picture of a _____ .

Say the words. Color the pictures.

heart hammer hamburger

hen hand house

helicopter horn hat

Which letter comes next? Write it in the box.

Example

A B C D E

1. B C D E

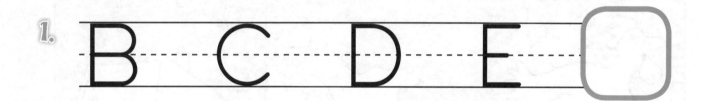

2. C D E F

3. D E F G

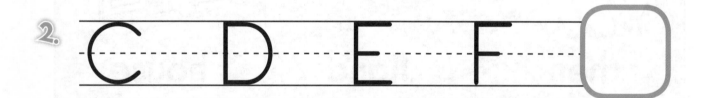

Date: _____

Which letter is missing in the sequence?
Write it in the box.

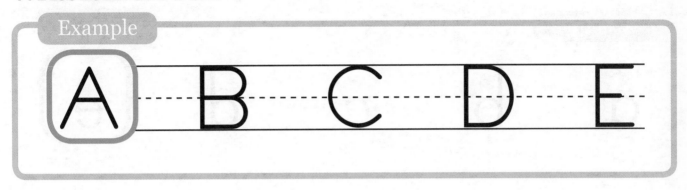

Example

A B C D E

1.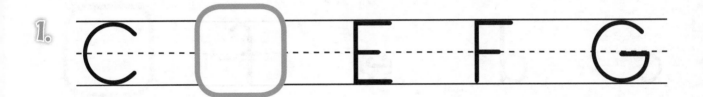

C ⬚ E F G

2.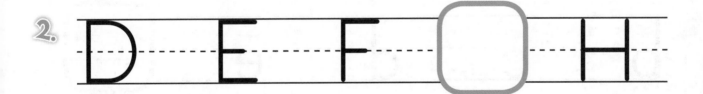

D E F ⬚ H

3.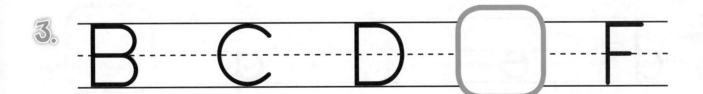

B C D ⬚ F

Date: _____

Which letter comes next? Write it in the box.

Example

a   b   c   d   e

1.

c   d   e   f   ☐

2.

b   c   d   e   ☐

3.

d   e   f   g   ☐

Date: _____

Which letter is missing in the sequence?
Write it in the box.

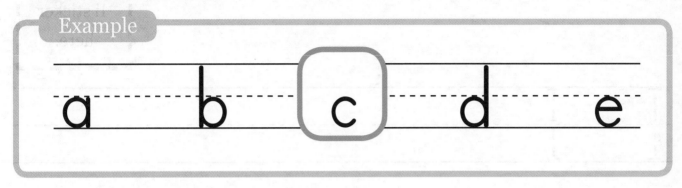

Example

a   b   c   d   e

1.

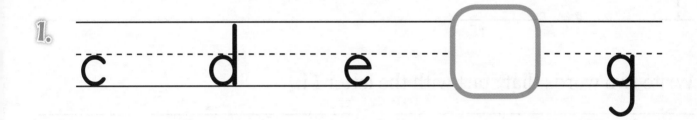

c   d   e   ☐   g

2.

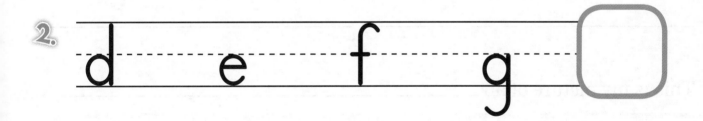

d   e   f   g   ☐

3.

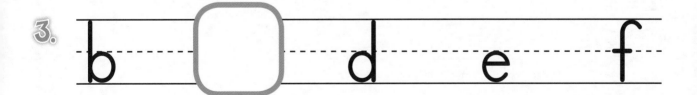

b   ☐   d   e   f

Date: _____

I am learning about the letter I i.
This is how I write it:

Write two words that start with the letter I i:

_____   _____

- - - - - - - - - - - - - - - - - -   - - - - - - - - - - - - - - - - - -

_____   _____

This is my picture of an _____ .

Date: _____

Say the words. Color the pictures.

ice cubes	ice cream	ink pot
igloo	instruments	iron
island	ivy	insects

Date: _____

I am learning about the letter J j.
This is how I write it:

Paste the
Jj sticker
here.

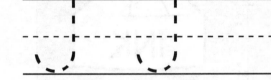

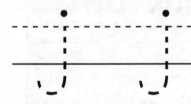

Write two words that start with the letter J j:

_____   _____

- - - - - - - - - - - - - - - - - - -   - - - - - - - - - - - - - - - - - - -

_____   _____

This is my picture of a _____ .

Date: _____

Say the words. Color the pictures.

jacket

jack-in-the-box

jar

jeep

jug

jam

jewelry

jigsaw puzzle

jump

Date: _____

I am learning about the letter K k.
This is how I write it:

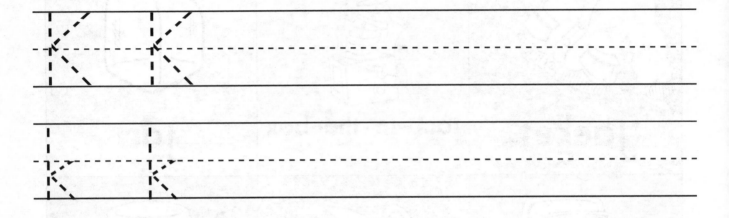

Write two words that start with the letter K k:

_____   _____

- - - - - - - - - - - - - - - - - - -   - - - - - - - - - - - - - - - - - - -

_____   _____

This is my picture of a _____ .

Date: _____

Say the words. Color the pictures.

kangaroo

kettle

keys

king

kite

kick

kitten

ketchup

KETCHUP

kitchen

Date: _____

I am learning about the letter L l.
This is how I write it:

Paste the
Ll sticker
here.

Write two words that start with the letter L l:

_____   _____

- - - - - - - - - - - - - - - - -   - - - - - - - - - - - - - - - - -

_____   _____

This is my picture of a _____ .

Say the words. Color the pictures.

log

lemons

ladder

ladybugs

lamp

lobster

lizard

letter

lion

Date: _____

I am learning about the letter M m.
This is how I write it:

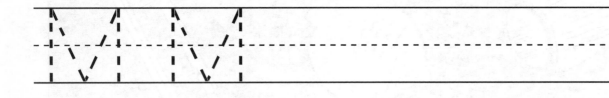

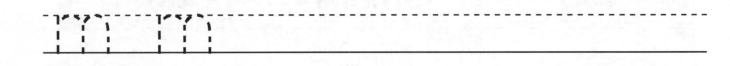

Write two words that start with the letter M m:

_____   _____

- - - - - - - - - - - - - - - - -   - - - - - - - - - - - - - - - - -

_____   _____

This is my picture of a _____ .

Date: _____

Say the words. Color the pictures.

mailbox

mask

mushroom

mittens

muffin

mouse

money

monkey

mirror

Date: _____

I am learning about the letter N n.
This is how I write it:

Paste the Nn sticker here.

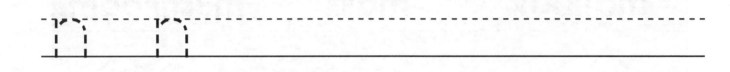

Write two words that start with the letter N n:

_____   _____

-     -

_____   _____

This is my picture of a _____ .

Date: _____

Say the words. Color the pictures.

nest

net

necklace

noodles

newspaper

nail

nuts

needle

nine

Date: _____

I am learning about the letter O o.
This is how I write it:

Write two words that start with the letter O o:

_____   _____

- - - - - - - - - - - - - - - - - -   - - - - - - - - - - - - - - - - - -

_____   _____

This is my picture of an _____ .

Date: _____

Say the words. Color the pictures.

octopus

oar

ostrich

owl

oil can

ornament

oranges

onions

oatmeal

Date: _____

I am learning about the letter P p.
This is how I write it:

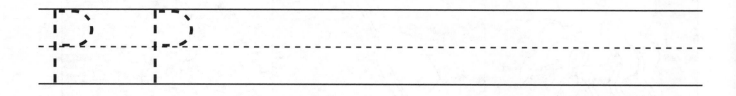

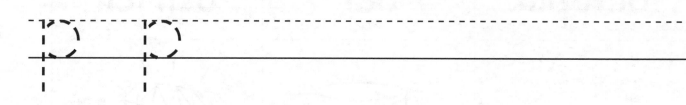

Write two words that start with the letter P p:

_____   _____

-          -

_____   _____

This is my picture of a _____ .

Date: _____

Say the words. Color the pictures.

pail

pancakes

parrot

penguin

pie

pineapple

pen

pumpkin

pyramid

Date: _____

Which letter comes next? Write it in the box.

Example

F —— G —— H —— I —— J

1. J —— K —— L —— M —— ☐
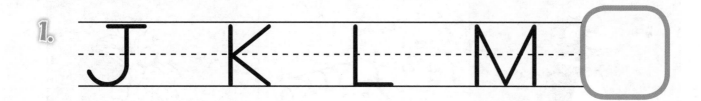

2. I —— J —— K —— L —— ☐

3. L —— M —— N —— O —— ☐
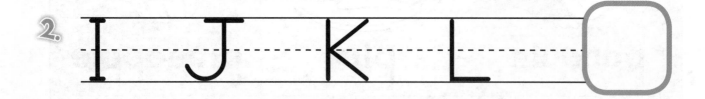

Date: _____

Which letter is missing in the sequence?
Write it in the box.

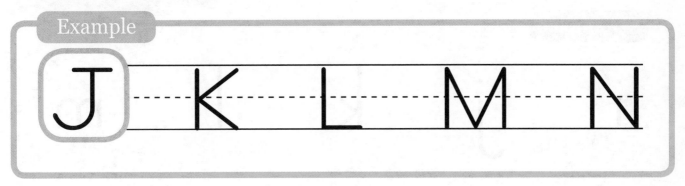

Example

J K L M N

1.

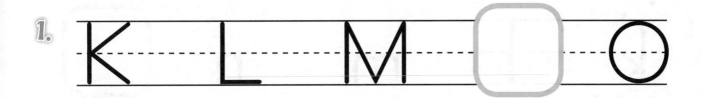

K L M ⬜ O

2.

L ⬜ N O P

3.

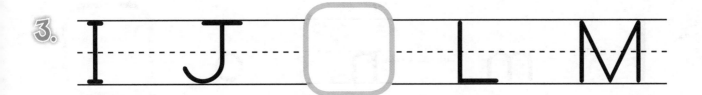

I J ⬜ L M

Date: _____

Which letter comes next? Write it in the box.

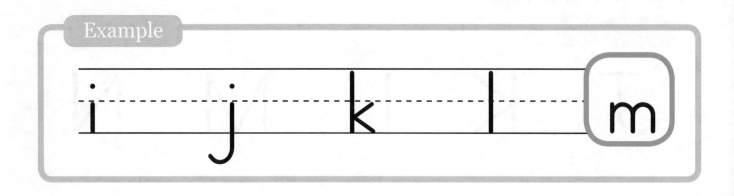

Example

i   j   k   l   m

1.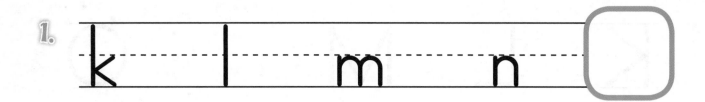

k   l   m   n

2.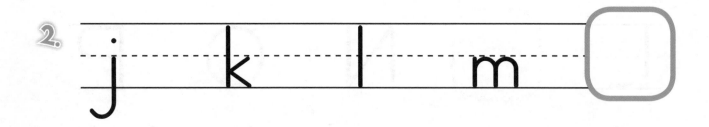

j   k   l   m

3.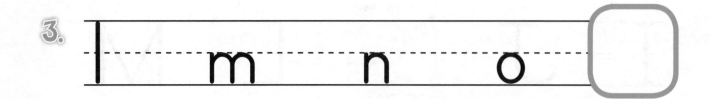

l   m   n   o

Date: _____

Which letter is missing in the sequence?
Write it in the box.

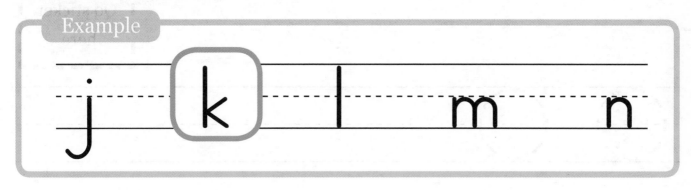

Example

j   k   l   m   n

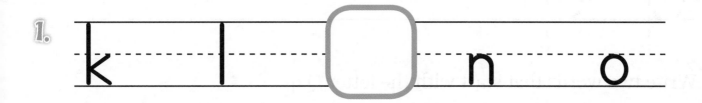

1.   k   l   ⬜   n   o

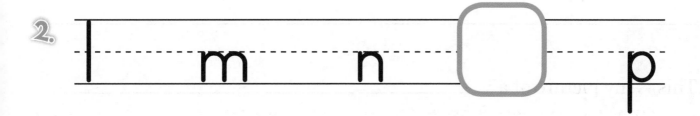

2.   l   m   n   ⬜   p

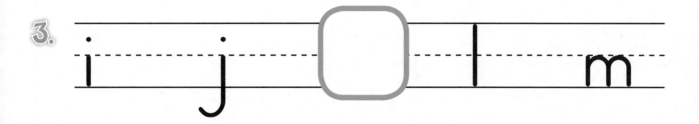

3.   i   j   ⬜   l   m

Date: _____

I am learning about the letter Q q.
This is how I write it:

Paste the Qq sticker here.

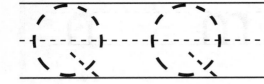

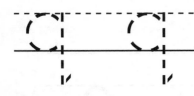

Write two words that start with the letter Q q:

_____   _____

- - - - - - - - - - - - - - - - -   - - - - - - - - - - - - - - - - -

_____   _____

This is my picture of a _____ .

Date: _____

Say the words. Color the pictures.

question mark

quilt

quiet

queen

quail

quacking

I am learning about the letter R r.
This is how I write it:

Paste the
Rr sticker
here.

R   R

r   r

Write two words that start with the letter R r:

_____   _____

-     -

_____   _____

This is my picture of a _____ .

Date: _____

Say the words. Color the pictures.

radio

rainbow

rabbit

rock

rocking horse

roller skate

rooster

rolling pin

refrigerator

Date: _____

I am learning about the letter S s.
This is how I write it:

Write two words that start with the letter S s:

_____   _____

- - - - - - - - - - - - - - - - - -   - - - - - - - - - - - - - - - - - -

_____   _____

This is my picture of a _____ .

Date: _____

Say the words. Color the pictures.

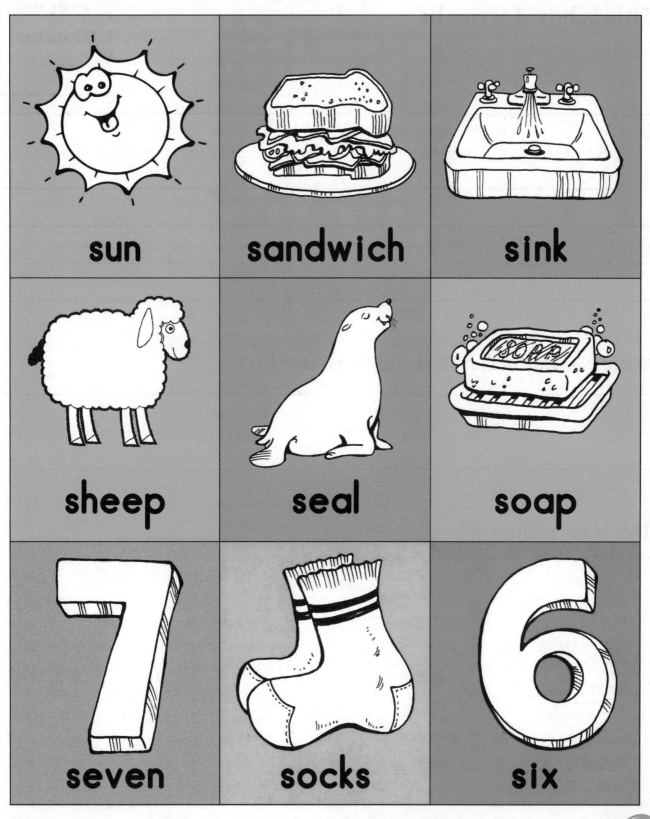

sun   sandwich   sink

sheep   seal   soap

seven   socks   six

Date: _____

I am learning about the letter T t.
This is how I write it:

Paste the Tt sticker here.

Write two words that start with the letter T t:

_____   _____

- - - - - - - - - - - - - - - - -   - - - - - - - - - - - - - - - - -

_____   _____

This is my picture of a _____ .

Date: _____

Say the words. Color the pictures.

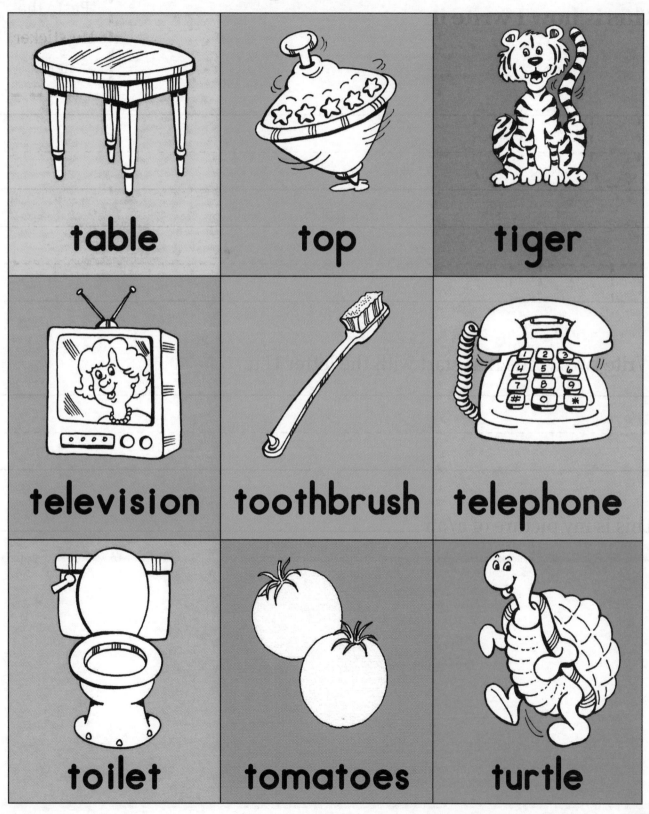

table

top

tiger

television

toothbrush

telephone

toilet

tomatoes

turtle

I am learning about the letter U u.
This is how I write it:

Paste the
Uu sticker
here.

Write two words that start with the letter U u:

_____   _____

- - - - - - - - - - - - - - -   - - - - - - - - - - - - - - -

_____   _____

This is my picture of a/an _____.

Date: _____

Say the words. Color the pictures.

| unicycle | umbrella | u-turn |
| unicorn | utensils | up |

Date: _____

I am learning about the letter V v.
This is how I write it:

Paste the
Vv sticker
here.

Write two words that start with the letter V v:

_____   _____

- - - - - - - - - - - - - - - - - - -   - - - - - - - - - - - - - - - - - - -

_____   _____

This is my picture of a _____ .

Say the words. Color the pictures.

vulture	van	vase
vegetables	volcano	violin
vest	video game	volleyball

Date: _____

I am learning about the letter W w.
This is how I write it:

Write two words that start with the letter W w:

_____   _____

- - - - - - - - - - - - - - -   - - - - - - - - - - - - - - -

_____   _____

This is my picture of a _____ .

Date: _____

Say the words. Color the pictures.

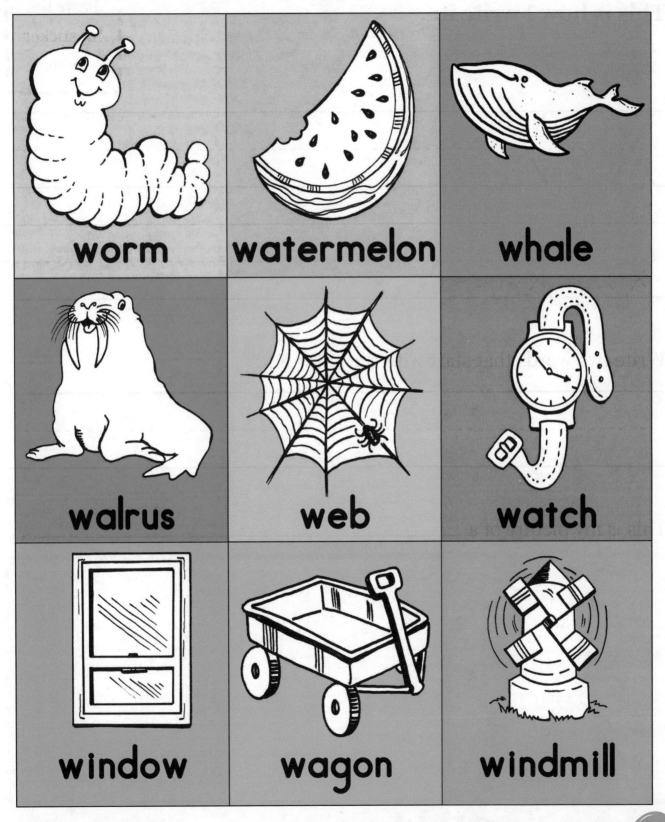

worm   watermelon   whale

walrus   web   watch

window   wagon   windmill

Date: _____

I am learning about the letter X x.
This is how I write it:

Write two words that start with the letter X x:

_____   _____

-     -

_____   _____

This is my picture of a _____ .

Date: _____

I am learning about the letter Y y.
This is how I write it:

Write two words that start with the letter Y y:

_____   _____

_____   _____

This is my picture of a _____ .

I am learning about the letter Z z.
This is how I write it:

Write two words that start with the letter Z z:

_____   _____

- - - - - - - - - - - - - - - - - - -   - - - - - - - - - - - - - - - - - - -

_____   _____

This is my picture of a _____ .

Date: _____

Say the words. Color the pictures.

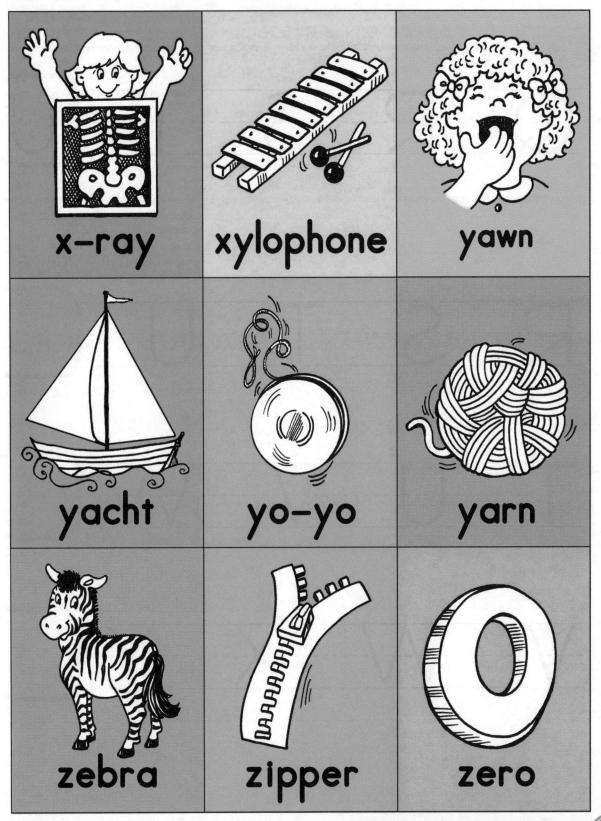

x-ray

xylophone

yawn

yacht

yo-yo

yarn

zebra

zipper

zero

Date: _____

Which letter comes next? Write it in the box.

Example

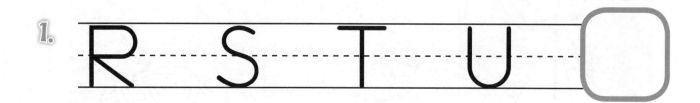

1.

2.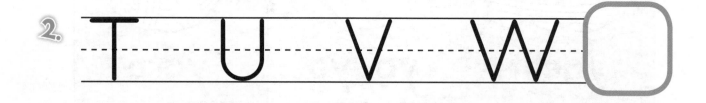

3.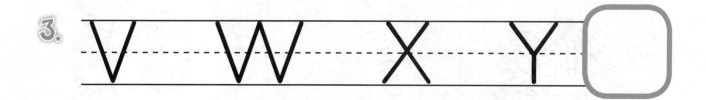

Date: _____

Which letter is missing in the sequence?
Write it in the box.

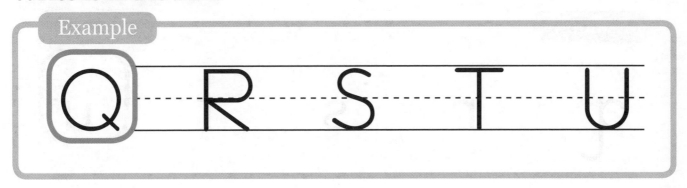

Example

Q R S T U

1.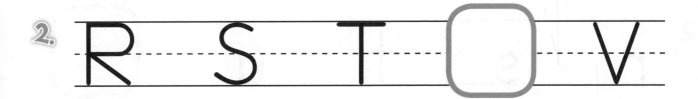

V W ◯ Y Z

2.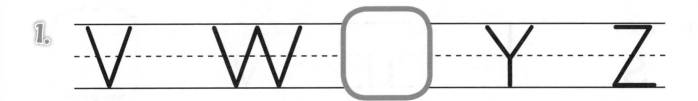

R S T ◯ V

3.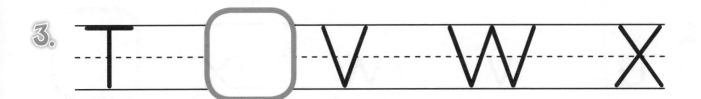

T ◯ V W X

Date: _____

Which letter comes next? Write it in the box.

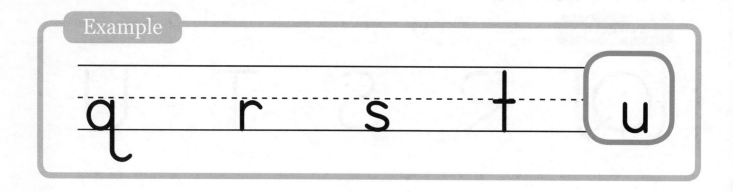

Example

q   r   s   t   u

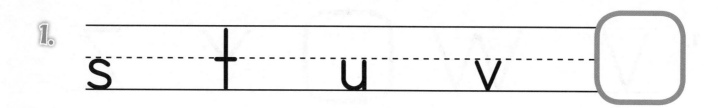

1.

s   t   u   v

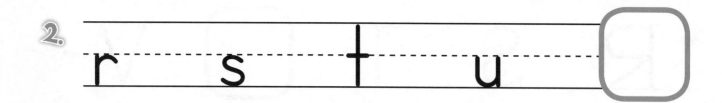

2.

r   s   t   u

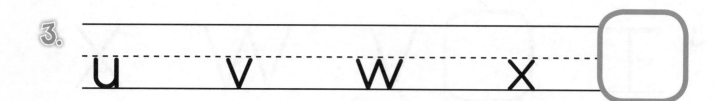

3.

u   v   w   x

Date: _____

Which letter is missing in the sequence? Write it in the box.

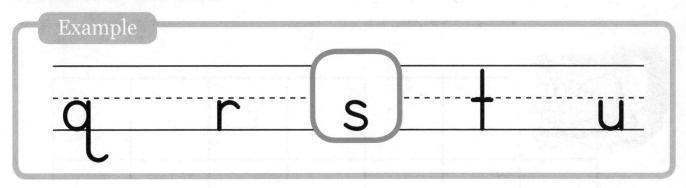

Example

q   r   s   t   u

1.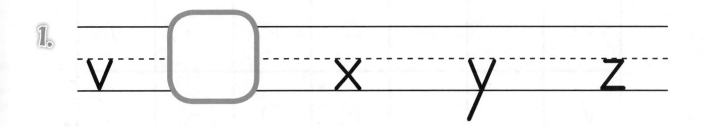

v   x   y   z

2.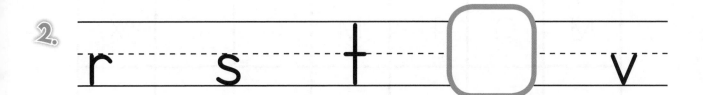

r   s   t   v

3.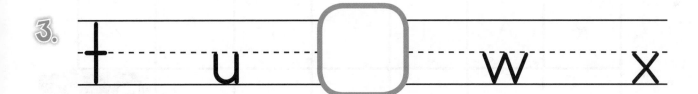

t   u   w   x

Date: _____

Help the rabbit find its way home. Color the boxes with the letters A-Z in the right order.

C	D	L	C	P	N
A	B	E	R	S	T	U
U	Y	F	Q	P	H	V
W	T	G	N	O	A	W
M	Q	H	M	G	C	X
P	V	I	L	E	D	Y
R	A	J	K	T	I	Z
K	L	A	F	S	J	

Date: _____

Help the mouse find its food. Color the boxes with the letters a-z in the right order.

a	b	c	d	f	r
t	v	g	f	e	a	c
u	s	h	o	q	t	x
m	g	i	j	k	l	m
b	s	r	q	p	o	n
c	t	u	d	e	t	e
e	l	v	w	x	y	z
t	v	t	s	u	v	

Choose the letters that come next? Color in the bubble next to those letters.

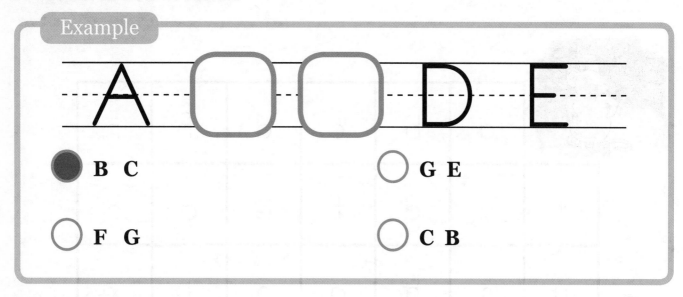

Example

A ◯ ◯ D E

● B C   ◯ G E

◯ F G   ◯ C B

1. G H ◯ ◯ K

◯ B C   ◯ I J

◯ F G   ◯ X Y

2. E F G ◯ ◯

◯ G L   ◯ Q H

◯ C K   ◯ H I

Choose the letters that come next? Color in the bubble next to those letters.

3. T U V ☐ ☐

○ X W   ○ Z Y

○ Y Z   ○ W X

4. ☐ ☐ O P Q

○ M N   ○ S R

○ L M   ○ R S

Choose the letters that come next? Color in the bubble next to those letters.

5. b ◻ ◻ e f

○ a c   ○ g h

○ c d   ○ c a

6. r s ◻ ◻ v

○ w x   ○ t u

○ p q   ○ w z

Choose the letters that come next? Color in the bubble next to those letters.

7.

i j k ☐ ☐

○ m n   ○ l m

○ n m   ○ g h

8.

p ☐ ☐ s t

○ o m   ○ m n

○ q r   ○ r u

Choose the word that begins with the letter in the box.
Color in the bubble next to that word.

9.

○ balloon   ○ lizard

○ jacket   ○ vest

10.

q

○ penguin   ○ guitar

○ banana   ○ quilt

Choose the word that begins with the letter in the box.
Color in the bubble next to that word.

11.

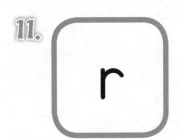

○ moon ○ arrow

○ hair ○ rice

12.

○ insect ○ lemon

○ unicorn ○ water

Choose the word that begins with the letter in the box.
Color in the bubble next to that word.

13.

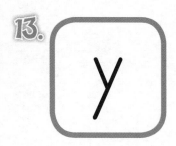

○ apple   ○ queen

○ igloo   ○ yacht

14.

h

○ kite   ○ dinner

○ bell   ○ horse

Answer Key

Page 6-21, 26-41, 46-63

Review letter formation, spelling, drawing, coloring and pasting of the sticker on each page.

Page 22

1. F   2. G   3. H

Page 23

1. D   2. G   3. E

Page 24

1. g   2. f   3. h

Page 25

1. f   2. h   3. c

Page 42

1. N   2. M   3. P

Page 43

1. N   2. M   3. K

Page 44

1. o   2. n   3. p

Page 45

1. m   2. o   3. k

Page 64

1. V   2. X   3. Z

Page 65

1. X   2. U   3. U

Page 66

1. w   2. v   3. y

Page 67

1. w   2. u   3. v

Page 68

C	D	L	C	P	N
A	B	E	R	S	T	U
U	Y	F	Q	R	H	V
W	T	G	N	O	A	W
M	Q	H	M	G	C	X
P	V	I	L	E	D	Y
R	A	J	K	T	I	Z
K	L	A	F	S	J

Page 69

a	b	c	d	f	r
t	v	g	f	e	a	c
u	s	h	o	q	t	x
m	g	i	j	k	l	m
b	s	r	q	p	o	n
c	t	u	d	e	t	e
e	l	v	w	x	y	z
t	v	t	s	u	v

Page 70-76

1. I J   2. H I   3. W X
4. M N   5. c d   6. t u
7. l m   8. q r   9. balloon
10. quilt   11. rice   12. water
13. yacht   14. horse